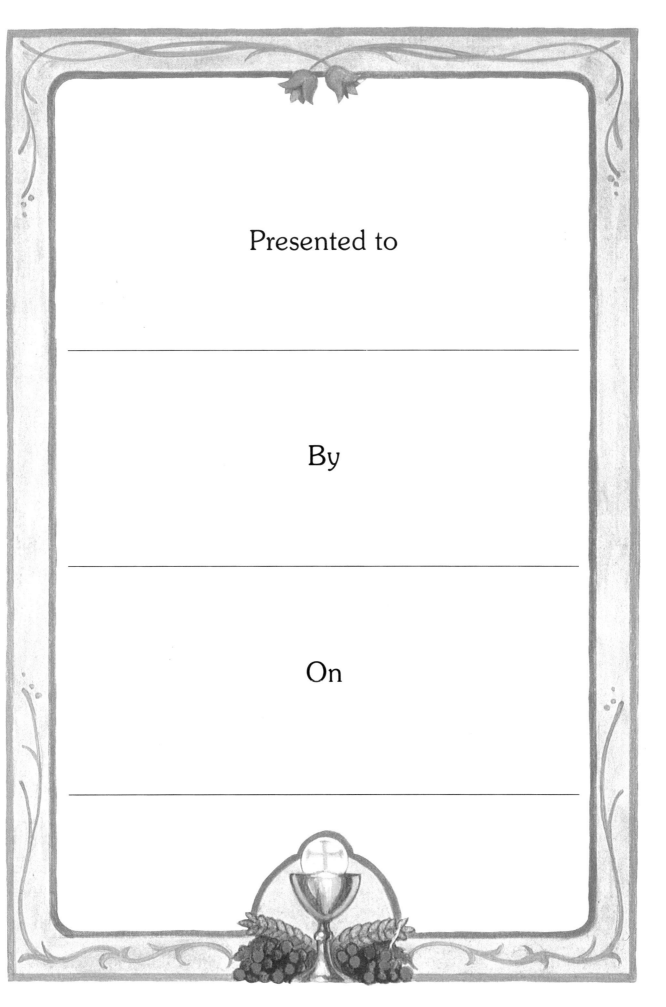

Presented to

By

On

Jesus said, "I will be with you all days, even until the end of time."

Remembrance of My First Holy Communion

Designed and Illustrated
by
George Angelini

The Regina Press
New York

My First
Holy Communion

_____

Received the Body and Blood
of our Lord Jesus Christ for the
first time

this _____ day of _____

in the year of our Lord _____

Church of _____

_____

_____

_____

Pastor _____

Jesus, I believe that I will receive you in Holy Communion. It is really you who will come into my heart and soul.

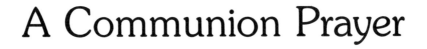

A Communion Prayer

Soul of Christ

(This is a prayer of Saint Ignatius Loyola.)

Soul of Christ, sanctify me.
Body of Christ, save me.
Blood of Christ, inebriate me.
Water from the side of Christ,
    wash me.
Passion of Christ, strengthen me.
O good Jesus, hear me.
Within your wounds, hide me.
Separated from you, let me never be.
From the malignant enemy,
    defend me.
At the hour of death, call me.
To come to you, bid me,
    that I may praise you
    in the company of your saints,
    for all eternity. Amen.

Jesus, I know you are God. Thank you for coming
to visit me. Stay with me always and be a friend in
my heart.

Jesus, now that you are within me, I want to ask you to bless my family.

My Relatives

Name	Relationship

Jesus, bless my friends, and especially those who
have no one to pray for them.

My Friends

Name

Name

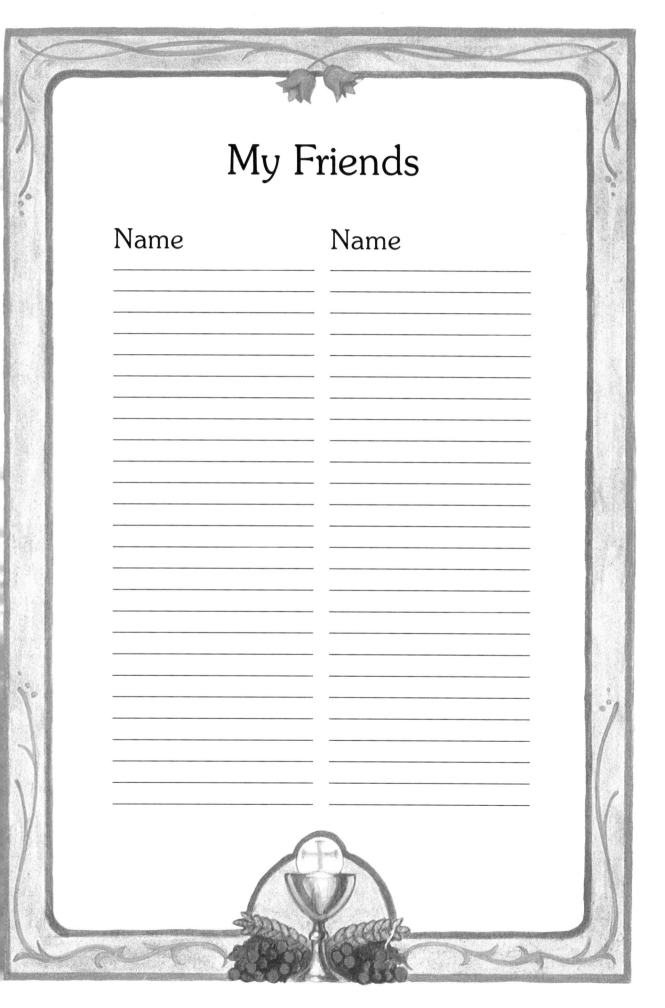

Jesus, see how much I need to grow. Make my
soul beautiful and stay with me always.

Gifts

Name	Gift

Important Prayers

The Sign of the Cross

In the name of the Father, and of the Son, and of the Holy Spirit. Amen.

The Our Father

Our Father, who art in heaven,
hallowed be thy name,
thy kingdom come,
thy will be done,
on earth as it is in heaven.
Give us this day our daily bread,
and forgive us our trespasses
as we forgive those
who trespass against us,
and lead us not into temptation,
but deliver us from evil. Amen.

The Hail Mary

Hail Mary, full of grace,
the Lord is with thee;
blessed art thou among women,
and blessed is the fruit
of thy womb, Jesus.
Holy Mary, Mother of God,
pray for us sinners now
and at the hour of our death. Amen.

Glory Be

Glory be to the Father and to the Son and to the Holy Spirit, as it was in the beginning, is now and ever shall be, world without end. Amen.

Act of Faith

O my God, I believe that you are one God in three Divine Persons: Father, Son and Holy Spirit. I believe that your Divine Son became Man and died for our sins, and that He will come again to judge the living and the dead. I believe these and all the truths that the Catholic Church teaches, because you have revealed them, who can neither deceive nor be deceived. Amen.

The Apostles' Creed

I believe in God, the Father almighty, creator of heaven and earth. I believe in Jesus Christ, his only Son, our Lord. He was conceived by the power of the Holy Spirit and born of the Virgin Mary. He suffered under Pontius Pilate, was crucified, died, and was buried. He descended to the dead. On the third day he rose again. He ascended into heaven, and is seated at the right hand of the Father. He will come again to judge the living and the dead. I believe in the Holy Spirit, the holy Catholic Church, the communion of saints, the forgiveness of sins, the resurrection of the body, and the life everlasting. Amen.

Grace Before Meals

Bless us, O Lord, and these your gifts which we are about to receive from your bounty through Christ our Lord. Amen.

Grace After Meals

We give you thanks, O almighty God, for all your benefits; you who live and reign, world without end. Amen.

Act of Hope

O my God, relying on your almighty power and infinite mercy and promises, I hope to obtain pardon of my sins, the help of your grace and life everlasting through the merits of Jesus Christ, my Lord and Redeemer. Amen.

Act of Love

O my God, I love you above all things with my whole heart and soul, because you are all good and worthy of all love. I love my neighbor as myself for the love of you. I forgive all who have injured me and ask pardon of all whom I have injured. Amen.

The Rosary

The Joyful Mysteries

1. The Coming of Jesus is Announced
2. Mary Visits Elizabeth
3. Jesus is Born
4. Jesus is Presented to God
5. Jesus is Found in the Temple

The Sorrowful Mysteries

1. Jesus' Agony in the Garden
2. Jesus is Whipped
3. Jesus is Crowned with Thorns
4. Jesus Carries His Cross
5. Jesus Dies on the Cross

The Glorious Mysteries

1. Jesus Rises from His Tomb
2. Jesus Ascends to Heaven
3. The Holy Spirit Descends
4. Mary is Assumed into Heaven
5. Mary is Crowned in Heaven

The prayers of the Rosary are The Sign of the Cross, The Glory Be, The Our Father, the Hail Mary and the Apostles' Creed.

My
Picture Album

PRINTED IN BELGIUM BY

proost
INTERNATIONAL BOOK PRODUCTION